Marine Biology

Cool Women Who Dive

Karen Bush
Gibson

Illustrated by
Lena Chandhok

GIRLS IN SCIENCE

Nomad Press
A division of Nomad Communications
10 9 8 7 6 5 4 3 2 1

This book was manufactured by CGB Printers,
North Mankato, Minnesota, United States
September 2016, Job #208069

ISBN Softcover: 978-1-61930-435-2
ISBN Hardcover: 978-1-61930-431-4

Educational Consultant, Marla Conn

Questions regarding the ordering of this book should be addressed to
Nomad Press
2456 Christian St.
White River Junction, VT 05001
www.nomadpress.net

Printed in the United States.

MIX
Paper from
responsible sources
FSC
www.fsc.org   FSC® C008080

~ Titles in the **Girls in Science** Series ~

How to Use This Book

In this book you'll find a few different ways to explore the topic of women in marine biology.

The essential questions in each Ask & Answer box encourage you to think further. You probably won't find the answers to these questions in the text, and sometimes there are no right or wrong answers! Instead, these questions are here to help you think more deeply about what you're reading and how the material connects to your own life.

There's a lot of new vocabulary in this book! Can you figure out a word's meaning from the paragraph? Look in the glossary in the back of the book to find the definitions of words you don't know.

Are you interested in what women have to say about marine biology? You'll find quotes from women who are professionals in the marine biology field. You can learn a lot by listening to people who have worked hard to succeed!

Primary sources come from people who were eyewitnesses to events. They might write about the event, take pictures, or record the event for radio or video. Why are primary sources important?

Interested in primary sources? Look for this icon.

PS

Use a QR code reader app on your tablet or other device to find online primary sources. You can find a list of URLs on the Resources page. If the QR code doesn't work, try searching the Internet with the Keyword Prompts to find other helpful sources.

CONTENTS

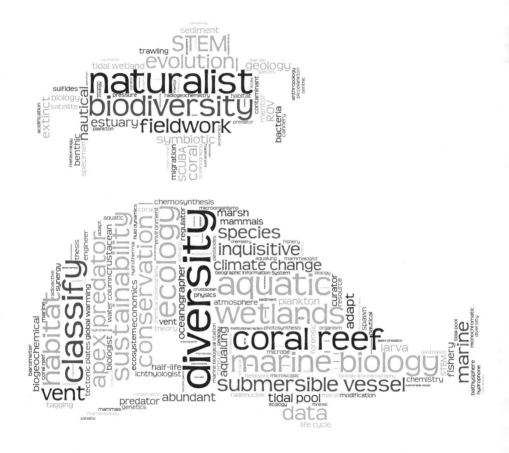

INTRODUCTION
The Mysteries of the Oceans

When you gaze upon the ocean, it looks as though it goes on forever. In fact, more than twice as much water as land covers the earth's surface. The National Oceanic and Atmospheric Administration (NOAA) estimates there are 321,003,271 cubic miles of ocean, or enough water to fill 352 quintillion gallon milk jugs.

Do you ever wonder how many organisms live in all that water? Scientists estimate that about a million species live in the ocean, but no one knows for certain because of the vast size and depths of the oceans. We are pretty sure there are many species that no human has seen yet.

Imagine discovering a new plant or animal. Maybe you'll discover a species that will lead to a new medicine or cure a disease. These are some of the things that marine biologists do.

You might know that the largest mammal in the world, the blue whale, lives in the ocean, but do you know that the world's smallest life forms also live there? Microbes may be small, but they are powerful. Marine biologists study aquatic life, from the smallest microbes to the largest mammals.

Blue Whale

Do you ride a school bus? Imagine attaching the front of one school bus to the back of another. The length of two school buses is the average size of a blue whale. On the surface of the water, the blue whale appears gray, but underwater, it appears blue, as this *National Geographic* picture shows.

giant blue whale
National Geographic 🔍

The greatest mysteries in the world can be found in the oceans and seas. Solving the mysteries of the oceans reveals what happened in the past and makes continued life in oceans possible for the future. Marine scientists collect clues to solve these mysteries.

In *Marine Biology: Cool Women Who Dive*, you'll read about three fascinating women who explore the oceans to try to find the answers to these mysteries. These women have worked hard to get where they are today, and they love sharing their passion for marine biology with others.

Lauren Mullineaux is a marine biologist and educator who studies the habitats and life cycles of organisms on the deep seafloor. Few of us have ever seen the creatures she works with.

66 What I loved most about being a research oceanographer was going to sea, especially the operational part: planning the expedition, figuring out how to work the ship, figuring out how to adapt to everything that happens while you're at sea and still come back with the data that you needed, and the accuracy that you needed. I loved that challenge. 99

—Kathryn Sullivan,
under secretary of commerce for oceans and atmosphere
and NOAA administrator

Marine life is affected by the chemistry of the ocean, and that's what professor and chemical oceanographer Ashanti Johnson looks at. She studies the chemistry of marine environments and how they are changing. She also shares her passion for science with students of all ages.

The ocean has always inspired marine biologist and artist Natalie Arnoldi. Her studies in oceanography and her talent as a painter are ways to explore the world around her. She uses both science and her art to ask and answer questions about the ocean and its resources.

The marine science careers of these three women show us that the ocean is a vast area filled with new discoveries and possibilities. In this book, we'll learn more about what they do and why. But first, let's explore the fascinating world of marine science that these women have chosen as their careers.

Ask & Answer

Why is marine biology an important career for women and men? What would science be like if only one gender worked at it?

CHAPTER 1

Life Is All Wet!

When you look in the ocean, do you wonder what's below? You're not alone! People have been peering into the ocean depths for thousands of years.

Marine biology is the study of life in the water. Marine comes from the Latin word *marinus*, meaning "of the sea." Biology comes from the Greek word *bios*, meaning "life," and *logia*, for "theory" or "science."

Marine biology concentrates on saltwater environments. These are oceans, estuaries, and wetlands. Estuaries are areas where rivers meet the sea. An example of an estuary is Chesapeake Bay in Maryland and Virginia. At 200 miles long, it is fed by several rivers and meets the Atlantic Ocean at its southern point.

Swamps and marshes are examples of wetlands. They can be freshwater if they're inland or saltwater if they're coastal. Coastal wetlands are also called tidal wetlands. Estuaries and wetlands contain many important marine ecosystems, which are communities of organisms that interact with each other.

The first marine life known to humans lives close to the surface or often comes up for air. As people built boats for transportation and to explore the world, their ocean voyages provided opportunities to see more species.

Knowledge of marine life expanded as explorers, pirates, and whale hunters kept journals describing the creatures they saw. These included seals, eels, whales, sea cows, and assorted fish. Captain James Cook (1728–1779) sailed the world twice during the eighteenth century, documenting the plants and animals he saw.

By the twentieth century, marine biologists were able to explore below the surface of the water with the help of submersible vessels and scuba diving. These advances in technology allowed marine biologists to observe and understand more about organisms that live in saltwater environments.

Sylvia Earle

Sylvia Earle (1935–) is a legendary marine scientist. With more than 50 years in the field, she is known for her work on marine algae, marine ecosystems, and conservation. *The New Yorker* and *The New York Times* have nicknamed Sylvia, "Her Deepness." She made her first dive as a college student and since then has spent more than 7,000 hours underwater. In 1970, Sylvia led an all-female team underwater as part of the Tektite scientists-in-the-sea project. The women successfully lived and worked underwater for two weeks.

In 2009, Sylvia was awarded a $100,000 TED Prize to "change the world." What do you think about her wish in this TED talk?

Sylvia Earle TED talk 🔎

MYTHOLOGIES OF THE OCEANS

Most cultures have myths or legends about the ocean. Sea gods, goddesses, and mermaids were often described as half human and half fish. The most well-known mythical sea creature was the Greek god Poseidon, who ruled the oceans. His son, Triton, was the messenger of the sea.

In ancient Babylonia, the sea god Oannes brought the arts and sciences to Babylonians. In India, the Hindu god Vishnu assumes the form of a fish to retrieve the Hindu scripture stolen by a demon.

In Inuit mythology, the sea goddess Sedna controls all animals in the sea. In order to keep Sedna happy, Inuit fishermen followed rituals, such as offering a drink of fresh water after killing a seal. If Inuit fishermen experienced a dry spell, the shaman transformed into a fish and swam to Sedna at the bottom of the ocean. He calmed her by combing the tangles from her hair and braiding it.

Chinese creation myths featured Fuxi, a god with the head of a man and the body of a serpent who could turn into a dragon. He was born in the Yellow River, the "mother river" in China. After creating people, Fuxi taught them to fish.

The ocean wasn't just a place for gods and goddesses. People also believed that frightening sea monsters and serpents lived below the surface.

Homer's epic poem the Odyssey tells of Odysseus sailing past Scylla, a six-headed sea creature that gobbles one sailor for each of its heads. Another sea creature, the kraken, was feared in twelfth-century Scandinavia. It had many arms, which it used to toss ships around in the sea or to pull them down below.

Many unusual-looking creatures live in the ocean. People may have suspected that the eel and octopus were sea monsters. Another candidate for mistaken identity is the bright silver oarfish, which is 25 feet long and has red spikes on its head.

A giant squid is an actual sea animal with 10 arms and many eyes, each as big as a soccer ball. It can grow up to 50 feet long. Does the giant squid sound similar to the mythical kraken?

Ask & Answer

If you lived hundreds of years ago and saw a creature with 10 arms and giant eyeballs, what would you have thought?

66 Everyone has heard of Jacques Cousteau, but how many people have heard of Sylvia Earle? Famous female role models in the sciences are often not as prevalent as men. 99

—Lindsay Aylesworth,
marine biologist

THE HISTORY OF MARINE BIOLOGY

Interest in the ocean is older than recorded history. Scientist Richard Ellis has said that the first marine biologists were probably fishermen or women walking along the shores gathering clams for dinner.

Fishing was important as a source of food and is a practice even older than farming. Ancient Egyptians fished from shore and from boats, much as people do today. They used linen nets, fish baskets made from willow trees, and hooks carved from bone, shell, and ivory. An Egyptian fisherman wrapped one end of his fiber line around his hand and tossed the other end with the baited hook into the water.

The first person to write about marine biology was the Greek philosopher Aristotle. He was fascinated with all nature, including marine life. Aristotle is sometimes referred to as "the father of marine biology."

Aristotle identified species of fish, crustaceans, and mollusks. In *The History of Animals*, written in 352 BCE, Aristotle noted that whales and dolphins don't breathe with gills as fish do. He knew that they give birth to live young just as mammals do.

After the thirteenth century in Europe, humans were hungry for knowledge and experiences. There was an explosion of ideas, art, and music. This time in history is referred to as the Renaissance.

Fish Art

Fish are common in cave paintings throughout the world. Many cave paintings are dated long before the first sailors. The world's oldest known cave paintings, located in Spain's Cave of the Castle, include paintings of fish. Rock shelters in Baja, California, show fish, marine mammals, and even manta rays. You can see some of these paintings here.
What do you see? Why do you think ancient people painted fish?

Bradshaw fish rock painting 🔍

A healthy coral reef
photo credit: NASA

Scientists, calling themselves naturalists, began asking questions. They began identifying and classifying what they saw in the natural world. In the early 1800s, the term *biology* began to be used to describe a branch of knowledge that included the study of living organisms and the processes of life.

Some biologists study life on land. Marine biologists study life in the oceans. Another word, a French word, is also used for ocean science—*océanographie*, or oceanography.

Edward Forbes from Scotland is considered by many to be the first marine biologist. In 1841, he theorized that different ocean animals live at different depths.

Coral Reefs

Reefs might look like rocks in the oceans, but they are actually living organisms. Reefs have an important role in the ocean's food chain, but they are at risk. Dr. Nancy Knowlton, a marine biologist with the Smithsonian Museum of Natural History, has been studying coral reefs for many years and has observed the changes firsthand. Each September, she visits the Caribbean coast of Panama to observe, document, and study the annual mass spawning of coral that can start new colonies and increase the genetic diversity of the reefs. What might affect the success or failure of the mass spawning? You can learn more about the health of coral reefs and see pictures of them at this website.

ocean coral reefs

Edward's experience with shallow-water animals, such as starfish and mollusks, led him to believe that nothing lived below 1,800 feet. While his theory about animals living at different depths has been proven true, it would take time and technology to prove he was wrong about life below 1,800 feet.

Charles Darwin, the father of evolution, studied and collected fish during his historic voyage on the *HMS Beagle*. He was particularly fascinated with flatfish, which are noted for eyes that move around during its development. Charles also published *Structure and Distribution of Coral Reefs* in 1842, in which he outlined theories about how coral reefs form.

Marine biologists sought to discover and collect new life in the same way that explorers discovered and claimed new colonies and countries. Specimens weren't arriving fast enough, so some marine scientists became explorers on ocean voyages.

The study of marine biology became more important by the 1870s, when people noticed they weren't catching as much fish in the Northern Hemisphere as in the past. Marine scientists realized that they needed to know more about the biology of organisms if fish were going to continue to be a source of food.

Ask & Answer

In the early days of marine biology, many animals were removed from their habitats and ecosystems and were destroyed so people could learn about new species. Do you think the results justify the methods? What would you have done?

> **66** . . . [as] great explorers and discoverers who charted and named the far corners of the world, scientists transformed the sea in the next frontier.**99**
>
> **—Helen Rozwadowski,**
> professor and sea historian

The 200-foot-long *HMS Challenger*, a small British warship built in 1858, was converted into the world's first oceanographic ship. It set sail on a cruise around the world in late 1872 with six scientists and 240 seamen aboard.

The *Challenger* was a floating science lab. Its passengers took samples of sediment, water, and marine life. Like other ships of the time, it used trawling gear to scoop up items from the ocean floor. We now know that trawling can be harmful to ocean habitats. Today, trawling is mainly used in midwater depths.

Traveling 68,890 nautical miles in four years, the *Challenger* visited every ocean except the Arctic. The ship came home with more than 13,000 plant and animal samples, which led to the identification of 4,700 new species.

As much as the *Challenger* achieved, it wasn't enough for many scientists. They knew that much more awaited them in the ocean depths. They only had to wait for technology to provide a way to discover more.

EXPLORING THE OCEAN DEPTHS

Like journalists who report on the news, scientists try to answer the what, where, when, why, and how of life. We now know that tiny organisms known as microbes were the first living things to appear in the water around 3 billion years ago.

Life didn't start on land, but in the water. Some life remained in the water, while other life evolved and left the oceans.

The first microscopes made it possible to see organisms in the ocean that couldn't be seen with the human eye, such as zooplankton and bacteria. Plankton nets with very fine weaves catch these organisms for study. Scientists now know that bacteria make up 98 percent of the total mass of organisms in the ocean.

Marine stations were established on land, usually on the coasts, to study marine life. People began looking for ways to go deeper by diving or traveling in submersible vessels. Without special modifications, the pressure of the ocean can make a person unconscious at a depth of 200 feet.

66 . . . a world as strange as that of Mars. **99**

—William Beebe,
describing the undersea world

The Age of *Aquarius*

Aquarius is an underwater lab operated by the NOAA in the Florida Keys. Scientists live in this underwater habitat 60 feet below the surface to study and observe ocean health and life. The *Aquarius* is also a place where both divers and astronauts train. The world on the ocean floor shares similarities with space.

One advantage of a 10-day mission at *Aquarius* is that scientist divers save time by not having to go through decompression every time they dive. Decompression typically takes 15 hours and 45 minutes for each trip underwater. Therefore, a marine scientist can do as much in a 10-day underwater mission as in two months of working from the surface.

You can see what it's like on *Aquarius* here.

tour NOAA Aquarius 🔍

photo credit: NOAA

The first successful submersible, created by engineer Otis Barton and scientist William Beebe, was called a bathysphere. It was made of cast steel 1¼ inches thick. The first bathysphere was 5 feet round and weighed 2½ tons.

With William inside, the bathysphere descended to 2,640 feet below the surface in 1930. He looked out the three windows made of 3-inch-thick quartz and saw marine life that no human had ever seen before. On a later voyage, he went more than 3,000 feet below the surface.

In the late 1950s, scientists and engineers began working on building larger submersibles. Each creation was tested by going unmanned into the ocean to see how long it would last against the pressure of the ocean, which could blow out the windows.

In 1964, a submersible named *Alvin* was delivered to Woods Hole Oceanographic Institution in Massachusetts. *Alvin* has been part of many adventures.

These include retrieving a hydrogen bomb and radioactive waste, as well as being attacked by a swordfish (the swordfish lost). It has been used by the U.S. Navy, geologists, biologists, and other scientists to study the ocean and marine life.

One of *Alvin*'s greatest adventures took place in 1977, when marine scientists took *Alvin* to the seafloor in the Galapagos rift zone of the Pacific Ocean. Until then, people believed that photosynthesis was necessary for life. Photosynthesis is the way sunlight is converted into chemical energy that feeds living things.

Sunlight cannot reach the ocean floor, so how could life exist there? Yet scientists saw life all around. Ghostly crabs, shrimp, fish, and 8-foot-long worms lived near cracks in the ocean floor. Inside these cracks are hydrothermal vents in the earth's crust.

Dive to the Edge of Creation

The discovery of the hydrothermal vents in 1977 rocked the marine biology world. Share in the discovery with National Geographic's documentary, *Dive to the Edge of Creation.*

Dive to the Edge of Creation 🔍

Normally, deep-water temperatures hover at the freezing mark, but near the vents, temperatures are 662 degrees Fahrenheit (350 degrees Celsius). This is hot enough to melt lead. Organisms near these vents produce energy in a process called chemosynthesis. This alternative to photosynthesis sustains life. Scientists discovered that life wasn't dependent on the sun.

At more than 50 years old, *Alvin* has had many overhauls. In fact, it doesn't contain any of its original parts. Today, there are better, higher-tech submersibles, but none have lasted as long as *Alvin*.

Human diving received a boost in 1943 when oceanographer Jacques Cousteau and engineer Emile Gagnan created a diving regulator to provide oxygen to divers so that they could remain underwater longer. They called their new device an Aqualung. Today, it is known as "self-contained underwater breathing apparatus" or scuba for short.

Equipment such as scuba and submersibles have made many things possible in the field of marine biology. Also helpful are remotely operated vehicles (ROVs).

66 Great attention gets paid to rainforests because of the diversity of life there. Diversity in the oceans is even greater. 99

—Sylvia Earle,
oceanographer

Robotics in the Ocean

As you can see, ROVs are invaluable for researchers. If you were going to build an underwater robot, what would you want it to do?

Deep Sea Robo Help 🔍

ROVs have been used since the 1950s to go where it's not safe for divers. These unmanned submarine robots transmit data through a cable and take specimens for further study.

In 2004, an ROV caught an image and a tentacle of a giant squid south of Japan. The 18-foot-long tentacle allowed scientists to estimate the size of the giant squid at approximately 25 feet. That's probably five times as long as you are!

Many early methods of studying the ocean disrupted ocean habitats. Today's marine biologists are careful that their research doesn't cause more damage.

Technology allows more research in laboratories and on computers. Fiber optics with LED lights and low-light underwater cameras can provide visual information about marine life species, behaviors, and life cycles. Hydrophones record sounds in the water. They not only capture sounds of marine mammals, but also the sounds of waves.

Ocean Census

Have you heard of the census? In the United States, the government counts the number of all its people every 10 years. The data from the census helps government agencies provide services and structure the government. Since 2000, a marine census has been documenting the diversity of marine life, including how many organisms there are and where they live. Approximately 2,700 scientists from more than 80 nations have contributed to the Census of Marine Life.

Never has so much data about the ocean existed in one place. You can see the data at this website. What information did you find most interesting? Were you surprised by any of the data?

census of marine life 🔍

One of the best tools is satellites. Satellites can track the behavior and movement of marine animals tagged with sensors. Changes in the oceans can also be recorded. Satellite data is downloaded onto computers, where it is analyzed.

The amount of knowledge about marine life in the past 100 years has increased dramatically. Yet it's estimated that only 5 percent of the oceans have been explored.

Additionally, global warming and climate change are leading to rapid change in the oceans. What else do you think oceans have to tell us?

MARINE BIOLOGY CAREERS

For today's marine biologists, the emphasis isn't on discovering new species, although it's estimated that there are thousands of species that haven't been discovered yet. Today, the emphasis is on maintaining and understanding current marine life. How much is there? Where does it live? How do we preserve it?

Marine scientists work on computers, in laboratories, and in the ocean. Many find themselves both teaching in classrooms and doing fieldwork. Research projects are often funded by a government institution, such as the National Science Foundation (NSF).

Marine biologists study the behavior, life cycles, and interactions of organisms within many different marine environments. They are often expected to publish the results of their research in technical journals and present findings to other marine scientists at conferences.

The term *marine biologist* can be used to describe many scientists in many fields that all impact marine life. In order to study and research marine life, marine biologists need the help of other sciences, including geology, ecology, zoology, chemistry, meteorology, and more.

Many marine scientists choose a specialty. Whales, dolphins, seals, walruses, and sea lions are popular subjects among marine biologists. A marine biologist or marine mammologist might study the habitat or behavior of these animals.

A marine microbiologist studies microorganisms, such as algae, bacteria, and viruses. This is how they learn what roles these microorganisms play in ecosystems and in the food chain.

Ruth Dixon Turner

Ruth Dixon Turner (1914–2000) might have started her education in a one-room schoolhouse, but she completed it with a PhD in biology at Harvard University. When the *Titanic* was discovered on the ocean's floor, people were dismayed to find that so little wood remained. Often, cold water preserves items. The world turned to Ruth for answers and she gave them. Bivalve mollusks, better known as shipworms, have an appetite for wood. They routinely damage boats, docks, and piers. Ruth was the world expert on mollusks, and her knowledge of shipworms helped people develop ways to reduce the harm they did. Ruth was the first female scientist aboard *Alvin* and was an accomplished diver who continued diving into her seventies. She worked with noted oceanographer Jacques Cousteau and was a Harvard professor.

Marine microbiologists also make discoveries. A picoplankton called *Prochlorococcus* was discovered in 1988 as the most abundant organism on Earth.

An ichthyologist is a marine biologist who studies any of the more than 20,000 species of fish, from small bony fish to sharks. Some ichthyologists work with or manage fisheries. Fisheries are like farms that raise fish and seafood for people to eat, and fisheries cut down on overfishing in the oceans. A fishery is also an ecosystem, and in order for it to be productive, it must be in balance.

A newer field within marine biology is marine conservation biology. Scientists in this field observe the ocean's health by finding and monitoring threats from industrial development and pollutants. A marine conservation biologist works in fields such as genetics, economics, and anthropology to come up with solutions to protect the marine environment.

Ask & Answer

Many marine animals are on the endangered list, and some, such as Steller's sea cow, are now extinct. What do you think the role of marine biologists should be in conservation?

To be a marine biologist, you should take lots of science courses in biology, earth science, chemistry, and physics. Math and computer science courses are important for collecting, interpreting, and presenting data. In college, you can major in biology, chemistry, or even engineering.

You don't have to wait until college to start preparing to be a marine biologist. You can start now by exploring the outdoors, whether you live by an ocean or not. All of nature has the ability to teach about biology. Train yourself to observe ecosystems and life processes around you. Be curious and ask questions.

Many science institutions operate special marine camps for students. Volunteering at zoos or aquariums is another way to prepare for an exciting life as a marine biologist.

Get Started on Your Research

The NOAA Pacific Services Center provides visual information services that collect data from around the globe. Choose one of the data sets and manipulate the globe to access the information that you need for your research!

NOAA global
science investigator

WOMEN IN MARINE SCIENCE

As with all sciences, women have made important contributions to marine science, but sometimes these contributions haven't been recognized.

Gender discrimination is when someone thinks a person can't do a good job because of their gender. Historically, women have been subjected to unfair gender discrimination and they have been prevented from getting jobs in the fields they want to work in. This is changing as women receive the same opportunities as men.

According to the NSF, women have received more than half of the biosciences degrees since 2009. At universities and marine institutions, women make up a significant portion of the marine scientists. Women are researchers, teachers, and leaders in the field. You can find them in the news, in documentaries, in newspapers and magazines, and on the Internet.

Let's meet three women working in marine science today—Lauren Mullineaux, Ashanti Johnson, and Natalie Arnoldi.

CHAPTER 2

Lauren Mullineaux

How do natural and manmade events affect the development of life on the ocean floor? What is necessary for ecosystems to develop on the seafloor? These are questions asked by Lauren Mullineaux, who is a senior scientist at the Woods Hole Oceanographic Institution (WHOI).

What do you think the ocean floor looks like? If you guessed dark, you're right! Sunlight doesn't reach the bottom of the ocean. There's also enormous pressure from all the water. It took scientists and engineers years to build a submersible that could manage the water pressure on the ocean floor.

Ocean Mountains

The ocean floor isn't flat. In fact, it contains the longest mountain range on the earth. Called the mid-ocean ridge, it stretches 40,389 miles. The mid-ocean ridge has formed from movement of the earth's crust. When the tectonic plates are pushed apart, magma rises up, filling the gaps and creating ridges.

That's where we find lots of volcanic activity. Volcanoes aren't just on land. Only 20 percent of volcanic eruptions happen on land, while the rest occur in the ocean. The Pacific ridge contains more active volcanoes because the tectonic plates are moving faster there than in other areas.

Marine scientists know that ocean volcanoes are sensitive to tides and gravity. They wonder if they are also sensitive to other changes, such as global warming. What do you think?

Early marine scientists exploring the ocean floor didn't expect to see life down there. But when a hydrothermal vent on the Pacific ridge was discovered in the late 1970s, scientists found bright red tubeworms, shellfish, and ghostly crabs among many other creatures living near the vent.

Sea water seeps into openings in the earth's crust and circulates. Water shoots out of these vents at scalding temperatures of 650 degrees Fahrenheit (350 degrees Celsius). The unique combination of minerals at the vents produces a process of chemosynthesis that allows life on the ocean floor to develop and thrive.

Hydrothermal vents only last for 10 to 50 years. Lauren wonders, what happens to marine life when a hydrothermal vent stops? To find answers, she started at the beginning of life on the ocean floor.

The marine life Lauren studies has two life-cycle phases, the larval and adult phases. Young juveniles, known as larvae, look very different from their adult versions. And sometimes you can't even see them without the help of a microscope.

Ask & Answer

What conditions do you think need to happen for larvae to successfully develop into adult marine life?

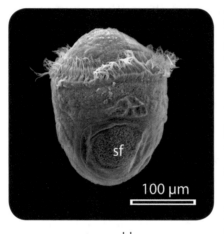

gastropod larva

photo credit: Daniel J. Jackson, Gert Wörheide, and Bernard M. Degnan

Deep-Sea Larvae

Larvae are similar to the seeds of a plant. Seeds need the right type of soil, moisture, and light to grow into plants. Larvae also need the right conditions to grow into adults.

Marine life isn't the only type of life with larval phases in their life cycles. You'll also find them with insects and some amphibians, too. Before you see a butterfly, it has been through its larva stage as a caterpillar. Like caterpillars and butterflies, marine larvae and adults don't look alike.

Take a look at the larva and adult stages of a gastropod, or snail. How are they different? Would you recognize these as being the same creature?

deep-sea gastropod
photo credit: NOAA

AT HOME IN NATURE

Lauren was born in Seattle, Washington, on June 22, 1958. Her family moved to Colorado when she was young and that's where she grew up. She grew up as a middle child among four children.

The family spent a lot of time outdoors. Lauren's mother was a naturalist who taught science to elementary school students. Lauren's father was a field geologist who studied the earth's rocks and minerals. Field geologists often work outdoors doing surveys on land in order to form a complete geological picture of an area. When summers arrived, the family would pack up the car and camp all summer while he did his research.

Lauren's parents encouraged curiosity about the natural world. She had lots of pets growing up, but she was also curious about animals in nature. Her curiosity took her outdoors in search of caterpillars, frogs, and insects. When her family visited the Pacific Northwest Coast, Lauren discovered new habitats—tide pools.

Ask & Answer

Have you ever seen an intertidal tide pool? What do you think happens to the animals in it when the tide comes in and then goes out?

Tide pools form at rocky shorelines where ocean and land meet. The tides cover and then uncover the pools each day. When the tide goes back toward the ocean, a variety of life remains, including sea stars, crabs, mussels, snails, bivalves, and barnacles.

Lauren credits an eighth-grade biology teacher for cementing her interest in living things. His classroom was often the outdoors, and science was a series of exciting discoveries. She's certain many of Mr. Sykes's students became scientists.

Tide pool in Monterey Bay, California
photo credit: NOAA

FROM DESERTS TO OCEANS

When it was time for college, Lauren chose a small college in California called Pomona College. While at Pomona, Lauren began to see science as an actual career choice. She wanted to better understand nature and how it all fits together.

She began studying ecology, which is the science that focuses on the relationships between living organisms and their physical environments. In particular, she studied the ecology of desert plants.

During college, Lauren took a cruise on a research vessel. It reawakened her interest in the ocean, which had started with those tide pools she had explored as a child. She saw many parallels between the ocean and the desert. Both are extreme environments. In both, the physical environments control the distribution of organisms.

After earning a degree with honors in biology from Pomona, Lauren began working on a master of science degree in earth sciences from the University of California. According to Lauren, she went through a record number of thesis projects before graduating! A thesis is a long-term project and paper on a topic you're interested in studying thoroughly during graduate school.

Another school in the University of California family of schools is the Scripps Institution of Oceanography. Established in 1903 as a marine biological station and place of learning, Scripps was the first school in the United States to develop an oceanography curriculum and a research diving program.

Today, the school offers programs in studies that relate to the ocean, including physics, chemistry, geology, biology, and climatology. Lauren earned her PhD in oceanography at Scripps in 1987.

Scientists with PhDs often embark on funded research projects to increase their skills and knowledge. This is known as postdoctoral research, or a postdoc. Fellowships are another type of post-graduate research opportunity. Lauren wanted to study fluids in motion, which are known as fluid dynamics. She was able to do this work in the ocean engineering department at WHOI from 1987 to 1988.

When an opening came up in the biology department of WHOI in 1988, Lauren applied and was hired as an assistant scientist. Since then, she has climbed the ladder in the biology department, from assistant scientist to associate scientist. Today, Lauren is a senior scientist at WHOI.

Woods Hole Oceanographic Institution

The country's oldest marine station, the Marine Biological Laboratory, lies on the Massachusetts coast. It was established in 1888. Today, it is part of the campus at WHOI. WHOI is an independent institution that works with education, government, and private companies in ocean research, exploration, and education.

Learn more about the people and work being done at Woods Hole.

Woods Hole Oceanographic Institution 🔍

Woods Hole Marine Biological Laboratory

Lauren describes herself as a biological oceanographer. This is different from a marine biologist in terms of the scientist's view and focus. A marine biologist generally focuses on specific species.

A biological oceanographer looks at the biology of the oceans within a larger context, such as a region. That biology can be affected by many different things, such as motion in the ocean.

Amy Bower

WHOI is filled with marine scientists making a difference. One of these scientists is Amy Bower. Like Lauren, Amy has a PhD in oceanography, but Amy comes from a physics background. She studies ocean currents and how the movement of water in the ocean affects marine life and climate.

Growing up in a coastal fishing town in Massachusetts, Amy was interested in marine life from a young age. When she went to Tufts University in 1977, she was the only woman majoring in physics. She attended a program presented by the Sea Education Association called Sea Semester in Woods Hole and discovered physical oceanography.

EDUCATOR

Lauren's days are spent teaching and researching. She loves both of these roles and would have a hard time picking a favorite. Interacting with high school, undergraduate, and graduate students keeps things interesting.

Students, particularly younger ones, ask all sorts of questions. Sometimes, Lauren doesn't have the answers. She loves the curiosity of students.

Physical oceanography focuses on physical conditions and processes, such as the properties and motion of the ocean.

photo credit: Tom Kleindinst, WHOI

While in graduate school, Amy was diagnosed with an incurable eye disease called macular degeneration. While she is legally blind, she still has some vision and doesn't let vision problems stop her. Adaptive modifications such as voice software and special computer monitors allow her to continue with the research she is so passionate about. She has published dozens of scientific articles and invented an instrument to better study the ocean.

Lauren has served as an education coordinator at WHOI. This role includes responsibilities with graduate admissions. WHOI and Massachusetts Institute of Technology (MIT) have had a joint education program in oceanography, applied ocean science, and engineering for almost 50 years. Lauren now coordinates the Woods Hole Summer Student Fellow Program each year.

Like all teachers, Lauren must set aside time to prepare lectures for the classes she teaches. These include biological oceanography, communicating ocean science, and classes on various topics in benthic biology and communities. Benthic organisms live in the lowest area of a body of water. She also meets regularly with graduate students, research assistants, and postdoctoral researchers about their current and future research.

Sometimes, Lauren's teaching duties take her outside of WHOI. She might visit local public schools or even universities in other countries. Lauren has been a visiting professor at Université Pierre and Marie Curie, a top public research university in Paris.

> 66 I think what inspires me is just figuring things out . . . coming in every day and thinking, 'Hmmm, nobody answered that question. I guess I better work on it.' 99
>
> **—Lauren Mullineaux**

OUT IN THE FIELD

In marine science, the field site is the earth. And there's nothing quite like marine science research out in the field.

Lauren sometimes feels like an explorer when she travels to places such as the East Pacific Rise. This is an area that lies at the boundaries of tectonic plates.

When Lauren first began ocean research, she was often the only woman on the ship. In a sense, she felt as though she represented all female scientists. She made certain she was productive and professional on these research trips, so that no one could have any complaints. Why was this important?

Today, Lauren says it's not unusual for half the scientists on board to be women. Often, a significant part of the crew operating the boats are female.

Lauren studies benthic organisms. These organisms live on the seafloor. Until recently, not much was known about them. Research on benthic organisms involves going out to sea and diving more than a mile deep in submersibles.

Marine scientists know that tiny larvae rise up in the water column for weeks or even years. The water column isn't a real structure.

Julia Barlow Platt

Julia Barlow Platt (1857–1935) was a marine biologist who used her knowledge and passion to save a polluted bay. Julia studied zoology and embryology at Harvard. Because she was a woman, she was unable to get a doctorate in the United States in the late nineteenth century. So, she moved to Europe. Julia earned a PhD in 1898 from the University of Freiburg in Germany. Although she had published 12 scientific papers, she couldn't find an American university willing to hire a woman as a marine biology professor.

Julia moved to Pacific Grove, California, a small community by Monterey Bay, in 1899. Overfishing and hunting of marine mammals had already taken its toll on the bay. The gray whales and sea otters that once frequented the area were gone. The bay was polluted with waste from canneries.

It is a way that scientists think about the ocean water as a series of layers, from the sediment at the bottom to the surface.

Larvae can't really move horizontally because of the current, but they can move vertically to get from one place to another. Each layer of the water column is affected by various chemicals, movement of currents, and other physical properties. Larvae eventually settle back on the ocean floor, sometimes near a new vent.

She started a petition to allow the city the right to manage its own coastline. No other California coastal community did this, but the state government approved Julia's petition. Julia started a marine refuge and prevented commercial fishing. Her goal was to create a place where larvae might be established and bring marine life back to Monterey Bay. Motivated by Julia's efforts, people began cleaning up the bay.

Abalone, sea urchins, and sea kelp prospered. This drew sea otters back to the bay in 1962 after more than 50 years of absence. Soon, the whales returned as well. Monterey Bay is now a prime whale-watching location. In place of an old cannery, the Monterey Bay Aquarium was established as a place to visit and for research.

How do larvae find the right type of habitat to colonize? Scientists hypothesize that the larvae are attracted by chemical signals from the vents. When and if conditions are right, larvae develop into adults.

The study of larvae also benefits estuaries closer to home. Commercial shellfish beds are located along the East Coast of the United States. Maintaining a productive shellfish farm is difficult. Larvae develop into adults only every two or three years. Lauren is studying the environmental factors that may affect the development and survival of shellfish larvae.

THE LADDER PROJECT

In order to study the ocean, marine scientists obtain grants from government and educational institutions. Common funding sources include the NSF and NOAA. NSF funded an important long-term project that Lauren has been involved with called Larval Dispersal of the Deep East Pacific Rise (LADDER).

The LADDER project involves a group of marine scientists from various educational and research institutions. Their objective is to investigate what influences larval movement and what leads to success in hydrothermal vent communities.

Alvin submersible
photo credit: OAR/National Undersea Research Program WHOI

At the hydrothermal vents, the hot water mixes with rocks, picking up sulfides and metals, such as copper, iron, and zinc. Microbes and bacteria develop in these conditions. Other marine animals begin life and form symbiotic relationships with the microbes. The microbes live on the animals and process the sulfides needed. In turn, the bacteria provide food to the tubeworms, clams, and mussels.

Lauren and her colleagues took three trips to the East Pacific Rise in the research vessel *Atlantis*. Then they used the *Alvin* submersible to get to the ocean floor. A chief scientist was assigned to each trip to oversee and lead the research trip. Lauren was the chief scientist for the third voyage.

How Does Climate Change Affect the Ocean?

Climate change affects the atmosphere, including temperatures and weather patterns. Did you know that it affects the ocean even more? Approximately 80 to 90 percent of the heat from global warming is absorbed into the ocean. This warming of the oceans risks all marine life. See this demonstration by a NASA marine scientist on what happens when warmer temperatures happen in the ocean.

climate kids
NASA ocean 🔍

The scientists sample and collect microscopic larvae for observation and experiments. In some marine biology research, scientists put sensors on animals. But larvae are too small for sensors!

Some larvae are no larger than the period at the end of this sentence. Lauren's research group has to find other ways to study these tiny creatures. They measure the current, take water samples, and collect larvae of different species.

The LADDER scientists set up experiments on the ocean floor. They have also sought to recreate the conditions of the hydrothermal vents with high-pressure systems in the lab.

With the systems in the lab they can culture and study deep-sea larvae. They also recreate certain conditions on computers.

Something that Lauren wonders about is how these deep-sea communities survive after a catastrophic event such as a seafloor eruption. This happened in 2006. While sailing near the East Pacific Rise, the team discovered a series of eruptions that had covered over previous communities.

Although this wasn't part of the original plan, the team rushed to the area. This was an opportunity to observe how larvae colonize new areas.

CLIMATE CHANGE AND THE OCEAN

Lauren's research has implications for the entire globe. Her European colleagues were invited to present at the 2015 climate change conference held in Paris. They wanted to make certain the ocean was part of any agreement.

Ask & Answer

Sometimes, scientists have to quickly change their plans to make the most of unexpected opportunities. What are other times that this is an important skill? Do you ever do this in your life?

For a long time, conservation efforts have been limited to what's happening on land. Marine scientists are trying to educate world leaders and the public about the dangers of climate change to the ocean.

The first world climate conference was held in 1979, but it wasn't until 1992 that an international treaty called the United Nations Framework Convention on Climate Change was established to limit global warming and address climate change. Since then, world leaders and environmental scientists have met each year. The 2015 conference was attended by 150 world leaders.

World Oceans Day

In addition to climate change conferences, people are bringing more attention to the oceans in other ways. One of those ways is through an annual event held on June 8. First suggested by the Canadian government, the United Nations General Assembly passed a resolution in 2008 to recognize World Oceans Day. Why do you think people decided to have a World Oceans Day each year? Learn more about World Oceans Day and see if there are activities occurring near your home at this website.

World Oceans Day 🔎

Lauren served on a panel on ocean and climate movement. She also presented her deep-sea research on larvae in relation to ocean acidification. Acidification comes from the increased levels of carbon dioxide being absorbed by the ocean.

Carbon dioxide is a greenhouse gas that is released into the atmosphere. It comes from the burning of fossil fuels and other events, such as respiration. Increasing carbon dioxide changes the chemistry of the ocean. It creates low oxygen and acidic conditions that larvae can't survive. If larvae die, what happens to the organisms that start life in this way? What happens to the marine life that eat these organisms?

The Paris climate change agreement, signed by 175 nations on Earth Day in 2016, holds countries accountable for their carbon dioxide emissions. A strong emphasis was placed on creating and improving clean-energy economies. Included in the resolution were statements about maintaining the integrity and biodiversity of marine ecosystems.

HONORS AND RECOGNITION

Lauren has received many honors throughout her career. She has held several important university positions in oceanography. She has also won the Arnold B. Arons Award. This award recognizes exceptional promise in teaching, advising, and mentoring at WHOI.

Lauren serves on committees for many organizations, including the NSF and a group called InterRidge. InterRidge shares resources for oceanic ridge research.

For several years, Lauren served as an associate editor of an international scientific journal, *Limnology and Oceanography*. The journal is one of the many journals where Lauren's scientific articles and research have been published. She has also written about deep-sea corals. Lauren now serves as a review editor for *Frontiers in Microbiology*.

Lauren is frequently asked to speak at conferences. Although benthic ecology and biodiversity are her main areas, she has also given talks on ecosystems based on chemosynthesis and deep-sea mining. Sometimes, those in her audience are leaders in government. More often, they are marine scientists sharing information to better understand marine life and the oceans.

Spare time is rare for Lauren. When she has free time, she spends it in nature, just like when she was a kid.

66 Even if you never have the chance to see or touch the ocean, the ocean touches you with every breath you take, every drop of water you drink, every bite you consume. Everyone, everywhere is inextricably connected to and utterly dependent upon the existence of the sea. 99

—Sylvia Earle,
marine biologist

CHAPTER 3

Ashanti Johnson

Jacques Cousteau was a French ocean explorer who brought the mysteries of the ocean through the television into people's living rooms. In 1976, he showed viewers the reefs and marine life from the Gulf of Mexico and Caribbean Sea. This episode of *The Undersea World of Jacques Cousteau* was one of more than 120 ocean documentaries by Jacques that gave most viewers their first look under the sea's surface.

Ashanti Johnson was six years old when that episode aired. Some day, she would see many of the sights introduced by the explorer. At a young age, Ashanti knew she would be a marine scientist.

No one was surprised when Ashanti went to college to major in marine biology. But a funny thing happened during her freshman year in college. She didn't like her biology class! She did, however, love her chemistry class. Ashanti changed her major to marine science with a focus on marine chemistry, and she has never regretted her choice.

Ashanti is a chemical oceanographer. She studies chemicals in the water, but often describes herself as a forensic scientist. Have you ever seen a television show where forensic scientists help solve crimes by collecting and analyzing evidence? Instead of a detective solving crimes, Ashanti is a detective figuring out what humans have done to marine environments. Her work has an impact on marine and human life.

> 66 It is a curious situation that the sea, from which life first arose, should now be threatened by the activities of one form of that life. But the sea, though changed in a sinister way, will continue to exist: the threat is rather to life itself. 99
>
> **—Rachel Carson,**
> marine biologist

GROWING UP INLAND

Ashanti was born in Dallas, Texas, on October 28, 1970. She is one of six girls born to Don Johnson and Vivian Williamson-Whitney. She wasn't the oldest or the youngest. She was in the middle. Ashanti was an active girl who liked being outside. She was also a fast reader who loved science.

In kindergarten, Ashanti was identified as gifted and placed in a special school. Her favorite television shows were science shows on PBS stations, including the Jacques Cousteau documentaries. By the third grade, she was fascinated with the ocean even though she lived more than 200 miles from the nearest coast.

In the summer after fifth grade, Ashanti's parents took her to Alabama to meet the daughter of a family friend. Beth Goodwin was a marine biology graduate student. Beth and Ashanti spent the day rowing in a boat and talking oceanography. Ashanti returned to school and did an independent study project on the differences between dolphins and porpoises.

Ask & Answer

Is it helpful to meet someone when you're young who is interested in things you might be interested in? Why or why not?

Ashanti attended the Dallas School for the Talented and Gifted. Every time a project was assigned, she focused on some aspect of the ocean. She quickly developed a reputation as a marine science nut. She even volunteered at an aquarium while in high school.

Rachel Carson

Rachel Carson (1907–1964) was born far from the ocean in Springdale, Pennsylvania. She grew up wanting to be a writer. After taking a biology class at Pennsylvania College for Women, she changed her mind. She discovered a passion for marine biology at WHOI.

In the late 1920s, Rachel started graduate school at Johns Hopkins University. She learned that, except for teaching, few opportunities existed for female scientists. Fieldwork was seen as too rugged for women. Despite these odds, and despite the Great Depression beginning two months after she started graduate school, Rachel earned a master's degree in marine zoology.

In 1958, Rachel began research into the effects of pesticides on the environment. Rachel's research showed that the pesticides entered the soil and water. She found links between exposure to chemical pesticides and stillbirths, birth defects, and some types of cancer.

No one, not her teachers nor her family, ever told Ashanti she couldn't be a marine scientist. Her parents told her she could do anything she wanted to do. Ashanti believes that having people who support you and being committed to your dream makes studying marine science within anyone's reach.

Concerned about the long-term effects of pesticides, Rachel's strongest message was that more research needed to be done on pesticides. She wrote a best-selling book about the problem called *Silent Spring* and appeared in a CBS special, *The Silent Spring of Rachel Carson*. Her arguments and science were sound, and people became concerned about pollution and the environment. The environmental conservation movement was born.

photo credit: U.S. Department of Agriculture

Sixteen years after Rachel died of cancer, President Jimmy Carter awarded her the Presidential Medal of Freedom. It is the highest civilian honor awarded by the U.S. government. You can see parts of the original CBS program in which Rachel speaks.

CBS Silent Spring 🔍

Dolphins vs. Porpoises

Ashanti's first marine science research happened before she was even a teenager! She researched and presented the differences between dolphins and porpoises. Not many people know the differences. Do you? Dolphins and porpoises belong to the same marine mammal order, Cetacea, from the Greek word *ketos*, meaning "large sea creature." Whales also belong to this family. Dolphins are more common than porpoises. They often have longer bodies and longer beaks. Dolphins have pointed, conical teeth while porpoises have flat or spade-shaped teeth.

Do you know what the largest member of the dolphin family is? Here's a hint!

A jumping orca

COLLEGE LIFE

When it was time for college, Ashanti chose a Texas school with an oceanography program—Texas A&M University at Galveston (TAMUG). The Galveston campus is one of 33 Sea Grant colleges. These schools are connected with NOAA and each other for the purpose of pursuing scientific research, education, and conservation of marine areas in the United States.

Texas A&M was the first public institution of higher learning to open, in 1871, in Texas. Its main campus is in College Station, between Dallas and Houston. During the 1960s, Texas A&M began formally admitting women and African Americans.

TAMUG is a branch of Texas A&M. Students there are called "Sea Aggies." It opened its doors in 1962, when it was called Texas Maritime Academy, and 23 young men were the first marine students there. The site included a marine laboratory that had opened 10 years earlier.

Ask & Answer

Marine biology wasn't what Ashanti expected, but she found a way to pursue her dream through marine chemistry. Have you ever been disappointed about something you were looking forward to? What did you do?

Beth Goodwin, Today

Since talking to young Ashanti years ago when she was 11, Beth Goodwin has taught marine biology, ecology, and scuba diving. She also takes people on whale-watching tours. Beth works for Jupiter Research Foundation, a nonprofit organization that develops marine technology to aid in the study of marine mammals. Her graduate degree is in physiology and behavioral biology.

Beth's true ocean love is whales, which she's been studying for more than 30 years. She and two other female marine biologists founded Eye of the Whale research to observe, analyze, and document humpback whales in Prince William Sound on the southern coast of Alaska. When they first began watching the whales, there were only about 3,000. Today, more than 20,000 humpback whales live in the North Pacific Ocean.

You can see photographs of some of the whales Beth studies at this website. Why do you think people are interested in learning about these huge sea creatures?

eye of whale research 🔍

During the 1970s, TAMUG added other marine science programs. By the time Ashanti started at TAMUG, it was a top-10 school among small colleges in the West. She became the first African American student body president of the school.

After receiving a bachelor of science degree in 1993, Ashanti began working on her PhD in chemical oceanography at Texas A&M. Ashanti's research project for her PhD involved studying contaminants in the Arctic Ocean. Her interest was specifically the Lena River estuary in northern Siberia, far from Ashanti's home in Texas.

This area in Siberia was the site of nuclear weapon testing in the 1960s. There was also a catastrophic nuclear accident at the Chernobyl nuclear plant in the northern Ukraine in 1986. Neither location was close to the Arctic Ocean.

Ask & Answer

Have you heard of situations where contaminants in water made people or animals sick? What do you think should be done when this happens?

The Lena River Delta

photo credit: USGS EROS Data Center Satellite Systems Branch.
This image is part of the ongoing Landsat Earth as Art series.

Ashanti discovered that each year, in the spring as the land thawed, nuclear contaminants entered the Lena River. They were transported to the estuary, Arctic Ocean, and even Alaska fisheries. The contaminants harmed the fish and the people eating the fish. She presented her findings at her first international conference and published her research in both the *Science of the Total Environment* and *Marine Pollution Bulletin*.

When she graduated with her PhD in 1999, Ashanti was the first African American to get a PhD in oceanography at Texas A&M. She was also one of the first African American female oceanographers in the entire country.

Radionuclides

In radionuclides, atoms contain too much nuclear energy. This makes them unstable, so they emit radiation. Radionuclides emit radiation at different rates. The time for half of the radioactive atoms to transform or decay is known as "half-life." Some radionuclides have half-lives of seconds, while others last millions of years.

The radionuclide that Ashanti studies most often is Cesium-137. This is a product of nuclear fuel that is produced during nuclear fission. A soft, silvery white metal, it changes form according to its environment. Cesium-137 moves through air and water. It is affected by temperature and can bond with other substances, such as clay particles. If Cesium-127 does join with clay, the radioactive material remains in the sediment. If not, it continues to be carried by currents and in the water column. The Environmental Protection Agency measures Cesium-137's half-life as 30.17 years. That means it can remain in the environment for a long time.

Exposure to Cesium-137 can increase the risk of cancer. Large amounts of Cesium-137 are not found in the environment. If they were, the substance could cause burns, acute radiation sickness, or even death.

CHEMICAL DISCOVERIES

After getting her doctorate, Ashanti received a postdoctoral fellowship at Georgia Institute of Technology. Later, she became a research scientist. Her research was on the radiogeochemistry in the ecosystems of estuaries.

Ashanti continued marine chemistry research, particularly on radionuclides that get into the water. This happens both naturally and through human activity. Radionuclides are radioactive forms of elements. Radioactivity changes the normal function of cells in the body and sometimes kills cells.

Ashanti's field research sites are often inland, but include coastal ecosystems in the Gulf of Mexico and in Puerto Rico. By analyzing chemicals and radionuclides in the water, Ashanti can learn many things. The chemicals tell her what has happened in the marine environment.

Ask & Answer

It was almost the beginning of the twenty-first century when Ashanti graduated from Texas A&M. Why do you think there hadn't been an African American oceanography graduate before her?

Cool Careers:
Marine Microbiologist

Marine microbiologists work with microscopic organisms from the oceans and coastal ecosystems. These are the bacteria, plankton, algae, viruses, and molds that live in the oceans at the bottom of the food chain.

Microbes are the most abundant and diverse group of living things on the entire planet, but they are quite small. Most can be seen only through a microscope. Marine microbiologists are finding that these tiny organisms have a huge impact on the health of the ocean and other marine life.

Whether working in the field or the lab, marine microbiologists research and analyze these tiny organisms to discover how they develop and what their impact on the ocean might be. Some marine microbiologists work in biotechnology. Some of the marine microbes may be the beginning of powerful and effective new drugs that will help people.

Marine microbiologists study biology, ecology, and biochemistry. Marine microbiologists have at least a bachelor's degree. Many pursue higher degrees in order to focus on specific interests and to qualify for more job opportunities.

The radioactive part works as a dating tool. It tells Ashanti how old the sediment is and when the contaminant was introduced. She can even discover the path the contaminants have traveled.

Her research helps people find ways to clean up contaminants. In the Savannah River estuary along Georgia's coast, radionuclides were found in the water. It was discovered that they leaked from upstream in the Savannah River where nuclear reactors were built in the 1950s. People are cleaning up the radioactive waste that spread to marshes and estuaries.

DIVERSITY IN SCIENCE

Ashanti's desire to help others realize their potential is just as strong as her passion for oceanography. She remembers how Beth and her professors served as mentors and helped her.

Early in her career, Ashanti noticed that there wasn't much diversity in the marine sciences. By choosing to be a mentor to students of underrepresented racial and ethnic groups, she is helping to change that.

She is also working to change how institutions exclude people of different races, genders, and cultures. The administrations at universities don't always realize that the way things have always been done isn't welcoming to all students.

The entire recruitment and admissions process could be unintentionally set up to exclude certain people. This is known as institutional racism.

While in college in the early 1990s, Ashanti spent summers as a chemist intern at Texas Instruments Central Research Laboratories. Each summer, a group of mostly African American high school students attended a program at Wiley College, a historically black college in Marshall, Texas. One of the activities was visiting the Texas Instruments lab where Ashanti worked. She talked to the students about chemistry, chemical engineering, and her interest in marine science.

Fast forward to 1997. Ashanti was attending a conference in Santa Fe, New Mexico, when a young African American woman approached her.

The young woman had been one of those students to visit Texas Instruments. She remembered Ashanti speaking to her class. Now, she was a senior at Hampton College, majoring in marine science. How do you think that made Ashanti feel?

Ask & Answer

Can you think of some examples of institutional racism? What are some ways to stop or reduce it?

Since 2008, Ashanti has served as executive director of the Institute for Broadening Participation (IBP). This is a nonprofit organization that is funded by NASA and the NSF. The organization is working to increase diversity in STEM (science, technology, engineering, and math) fields.

This community of scientists helps students with fellowships, internships, and scholarships. Under the IBP umbrella is another program Ashanti established, called Minorities Striving and Pursuing Higher Degrees of Success in Earth System Science Initiative.

Mentoring

Working with young people is an important part of Ashanti's identity as a scientist. She feels that her own career was inspired by the women she knew as a young girl who believed in her ability to be an oceanographer. Part of her role, she feels, is to help others find a path toward their career goals. You can hear her talk about her experiences and her work with IBP here.

Ashanti Johnson
IBP video 🔍

EDUCATOR

Like many marine scientists, Ashanti also teaches. She taught at Georgia Institute of Technology and Savannah State University. After a couple of years, she moved to the University of South Florida as an assistant professor in the College of Marine Science. About 65 percent of her time was spent writing proposals and scientific papers. She has proven to be good at securing federal funding for research projects.

She taught marine chemistry courses in topics such as radiogeochemistry and biogeochemical sensors. She also taught a STEM professional development course to prepare graduate students for careers in the sciences. Assisting minority graduate students in STEM areas find funding for education has also been important to her.

In 2013, Ashanti moved back to Texas as an associate professor of earth and environmental sciences at University of Texas at Arlington. In addition to teaching environmental science and STEM professional development, she has a role in faculty recruitment and as a faculty research associate.

Ashanti continues in her position as executive director of IBP. Although the main office is located in Maine, a regional office opened at the University of Texas at Arlington. Ashanti's time is almost evenly split between marine science and diversity work.

HONORS AND AWARDS

Ashanti has received numerous honors and awards. While in school, she was named the American Geological Institute Minority Graduate Scholar. She is often recognized for her work in promoting STEM and diversity.

Kakani Katija

Kakani Katija (1983–) is a bioengineer who studies motion in the ocean. The motion may be caused by ocean currents, but Kakani believes it is also caused by marine animals.

Remember the water column mentioned in the previous chapter? These layers of ocean water contain different temperatures, pressures, and levels of saline. Ocean layers mix, but Kakani doesn't think it's just tides and currents that cause the mixing. Work in the lab has shown that smaller creatures may influence the mixing more than we ever knew. Small fish and marine creatures have the highest population numbers—sometimes, there are as many as thousands per square yard! With millions of animals moving up and down in the ocean to find food every day, their motion may mix the ocean.

Kakani travels around the world to observe and analyze the effects of large marine populations on the mixing of ocean layers.

While working at the University of South Florida in 2008, Ashanti was one of 20 educators throughout the nation chosen to receive the Presidential Award for Excellence in Science, Mathematics and Engineering Mentoring, given by President Barack Obama.

This type of work requires Kakani to do lots of diving. She and her team record and measure the flow of water around animals with special cameras and fluorescent dyes. Her research could tell us more about the effects of climate change on the ocean.

As an engineer, Kakani has also observed the various forms of propulsion that marine life use to move through water. Perhaps she will be able to duplicate marine animal movements. This might help engineers design more efficient devices for humans to use when they move around in the deep sea or even when they move around on land. Why is it useful to get ideas for human tools from nature?

Cool Careers:
Marine Geologist

Like chemistry, geology is an important marine science. Marine geologists study the structure of the ocean floor, including the rocks and sediments. They look at plate tectonics and how the ocean floors are always growing and shifting.

The active volcano area with high seismic activity in the Pacific that's often called the Ring of Fire is a popular place to study. Studying rock formations can tell us a lot about the history of an area and its age.

Marine geologists have to do a lot of fieldwork, including diving in submersibles to the ocean floor. Physical oceanographers, marine geophysicists, and geochemists are other types of scientists who study the structures of the ocean floor.

People interested in marine geology often study oceanography or geology as undergraduates. When they go to graduate school, they specialize in marine geology.

Ashanti is often featured in interviews for her work. She is also recognized during African American History and Women's History months for being a role model. TheGrio.com recognized her as one of 100 "History Makers in the Making."

Like many researchers, Ashanti has published her research in scientific journals, including *American Scientist* and the *Journal of Environmental Science and Engineering*. She also presents on both marine science and diversity at conferences.

Ashanti stays busy as a chemical oceanographer and educator. When she's not working, she enjoys spending time with her three children. She calls them her water babies because they love beach vacations as much as she does. Her family stays active by snorkeling, scuba diving, and exploring the ocean.

> 66 Being attracted to science is cool. It's a neat thing. You can still be a girl and involved in science. And when you get into different positions of success, you can help other young people, which is something I'm committed to. 99
>
> **—Ashanti Johnson**

CHAPTER 4

Natalie Arnoldi

Natalie Arnoldi is a marine biologist who studies sharks. She remembers being fascinated by sharks even as a child. There was just something thrilling about a large fish that could eat you whole! And if the popularity of Discovery Channel's *Shark Week* is any indication, she's not alone. The 2015 season of the show had 2.5 million viewers. Were you one of them?

How do you think the leopard shark got its name?

Sharks are among the oldest species in the oceans, and one that inspires fear in many. Sharks have been around for at least 418 million years. Those early sharks don't look very much like today's sharks. For one thing, prehistoric sharks were much smaller.

The average prehistoric shark was about 9 inches long with one-eighth-inch-long teeth. Small sharks, such as the spined pygmy shark, still exist today. But more of today's sharks are as long as adult humans are tall. Great white sharks, which were immortalized in the *Jaws* movies, are two or three times larger than humans.

> **66** I never let being a woman—even as a young girl—stop me from trying to do something I really wanted to do, especially if it concerned fishes or the underwater world. **99**
>
> **—Eugenie Clark,**
> ichthyologist, marine biologist

A LIFE BY THE OCEAN

The ocean has always been a part of Natalie's life, and she can't imagine it any other way. Born in Santa Monica, California, on July 16, 1990, she grew up on the beaches of Malibu and Venice. During her childhood, she spent a lot of time outside exploring what the ocean had to offer.

Shark Week

Shark Week debuted in 1988. By 2013, it resembled the *Jaws* movies with a focus on stunts and gore. While it had a large viewing audience, there were complaints about the content. A change in leadership led to changes in 2015 with more of a focus on science, biodiversity, and conservation. It worked. *Shark Week* was the highest-rated cable television show in July 2015.

More than 400 species of sharks live in oceans around the world, and, as Natalie has learned, sharks are interesting for many reasons. For one, they continuously grow teeth. Can you imagine getting a new set of teeth every 7 to 10 days?

Natalie's parents, Charles and Katie, always encouraged Natalie and her older brother to question the world around them and create their own unique perspectives. Katie is a novelist whose work has been featured on the *Los Angeles Times* bestseller lists. Charles is a well-known painter and sculptor. His work hangs in museums and galleries around the world.

Eugenie Clark

Natalie is not the first female marine biologist to be fascinated by sharks, and she certainly won't be the last. Most people credit Eugenie Clark (1922–2015) as the first. She was nicknamed "Shark Lady." Like Natalie, Eugenie discovered the wonder of sharks as a young child.

Eugenie was born in New York City to a Japanese mother and an American father. Eugenie believes her Japanese culture inspired her interest in the ocean. She described the Japanese culture as more ocean-focused.

Eugenie "Shark Lady" Clark
photo credit: Mote Marine Laboratory

Natalie's first close encounter with sharks was around the age of seven or eight. While snorkeling near her home, she saw schools of leopard sharks carpeting the ocean floor.

Leopard sharks often feed in the tidal and bay areas of North America's Pacific Coast. Unlike the great white shark, leopard sharks are not threatening or dangerous at all.

Eugenie learned to swim soon after walking. Her favorite place to go was the New York Aquarium. She used to wonder what it would be like to swim with the creatures she saw there.

In the 1940s, Eugenie studied ichthyology, the science of fish, at Hunter College. Later, she earned a PhD at New York University. She had wanted to do her postdoctoral work at Columbia University.

One of the scientists at Columbia said it would be a waste of the university's time and money because she would probably just get married and have children instead of using her knowledge. Eugenie did it all—marriage, children, and marine biology. She took more than 70 dives in submersibles. She died eight months after her last scuba dive at the age of 92.

Watch this 1982 National Geographic documentary where she talks about sharks.

National Geographic video
The Sharks 1982 🔎

Cool Careers:
Ichthyologist

Ichthyology is the science of fish. It includes their history, behavior, biology, and ecosystems. Many ichthyologists focus on a specific species of fish. Others study various kinds of fish or fish in a specific geographical area. Like other marine scientists, ichthyologists do field research to observe and collect samples. They may also work in a lab to analyze and report on data. If their job is connected to a university, they might teach as well.

Ichthyologists work in aquariums, museums, fisheries, and for the government. Most jobs for ichthyologists in the United States are located in coastal areas. The largest number of ichthyologists are based in California, followed by Washington and Florida.

Entry-level ichthyologists usually have a bachelor's degree in marine biology, marine ecology, zoology, or a related marine science. Many ichthyologists continue their education and get master's and doctorate degrees.

Snorkeling, surfing, and living life by the ocean were regular activities in the Arnoldi household. Natalie even worked as a junior lifeguard.

While in high school, she was an aquarist intern at Heal the Bay at Santa Monica Pier Aquarium. Heal the Bay is a public marine education center. Natalie's job duties included taking care of the animals and educating visitors about the marine environment.

Charles and Katie Arnoldi taught their children to explore the world in a creative way and to follow their passions. Natalie applied that to marine science. A high school marine biology teacher also encouraged Natalie's pursuit of marine science.

OFF TO COLLEGE

Natalie took her curiosity about sharks to college at Stanford University, where it was only natural to major in marine biology. She learned more about the ocean's large predators. These include sharks, as well as tuna and billfish.

She continued her studies as a graduate student. Natalie graduated with a master of science degree in earth systems in 2014, specializing in oceanography and marine policy.

Stanford marine science graduate students spend time doing fieldwork on research and thesis projects. They might do research at Hopkins Marine Station, aboard research vessels, and even in other countries. Natalie's studies took her to Australia in 2011.

Hopkins Marine Station is Stanford's marine science lab, located in Monterey, California. Although it's located 90 miles south of the main campus, it serves a large number of researchers, plus undergraduate and graduate students. Hopkins also uses research vessels such as the *SSV Robert C. Seamans* to do fieldwork in the Pacific Ocean.

Natalie's last year of graduate school included working as a teaching assistant. She developed and taught an introductory environmental science course. She also took on the role of educator at Stanford at Sea, where she taught a conservation course and advanced principles of marine biology.

Stanford@SEA is a 16-unit oceanography course at Stanford University. Half of the course takes place at Hopkins Marine Station, where students learn about oceanography, crewing for a research ship, and developing a research program. The other half of the course takes place in the Pacific Ocean aboard the research vessel *Robert C. Seamans.*

For five weeks, students focus on research projects and sailing the ship while on the open sea.

They also continue taking courses to deepen their understanding of oceanographic research.

Stanford@SEA isn't just for marine science students. Students with other majors apply, too, including those studying engineering, international relations, and more. The ocean has an impact on everything.

Many university degree programs require their graduate students to complete a research paper known as a thesis. Natalie was an honors recipient for her thesis on salmon sharks in the California Current.

California Current

What is the California Current and why is it so important? This current follows the west coast of the United States, moving cool water south. Because of the colder, nutrient-rich waters below the surface, large populations of marine animals live in the North Pacific, including whales and seabirds. The California Current is an ecosystem with an abundance and diversity of marine life that draws migratory species each year. It is a prime location for fisheries. The California Current aids scientists in studying the effects of climate change related to El Niño, too.

The salmon shark lives in the North Pacific. It gets its name from being one of the chief predators of Pacific salmon. Natalie's paper examined patterns of salmon shark presence in the California Current and how those patterns relate to oceanographic seasons.

When she was in school, Natalie noticed more female marine biology students. While science is still dominated by men, Natalie knows of many hugely influential female marine scientists, including her undergraduate advisor, Barbara Block.

Barbara Block

Natalie's undergraduate advisor, Barbara Block, understands all about large predators and their role in ecosystems. With a PhD from Duke University, Barbara is one of the world's most noted experts on the second-largest fish in the ocean, the bluefin tuna. Her research has shown that these warm-blooded fish can migrate thousands of miles. In addition to her work with bluefin tuna, Barbara is the Charles and Elizabeth Prothro Professor in Marine Sciences in the department of biology at Stanford. Her lab is located at Stanford's Hopkins Marine Station. She also works with the Monterey Bay Aquarium Tuna Research and Conservation Center. You can hear more about her work in this TED talk.

Barbara Block TED talk
tagging tuna 🔍

THE IMPORTANCE OF DATA

When Natalie was five years old, the first worldwide mapping of the seafloor was created from GEOSAT satellite radar altimetry data. The size of the ocean and the physical difficulty in reaching some places makes electronic data invaluable in marine science.

Much of marine biology is data collection and analysis. Technology such as ArcGIS, MATLAB, and satellite data aid marine biologists in finding answers to questions. Numbers reveal patterns that help us understand marine life and the ocean.

Geographic Information Systems (GIS) are used by government, businesses, and the general public. GIS uses satellite data for mapping capabilities. The data from GIS also allows users to see, analyze, and interpret data for their needs.

Ask & Answer

A mentor is a knowledgeable person who advises someone, just as Barbara advised Natalie. Have you ever had a mentor? If so, how did your mentor help you?

ArcGIS by Esri is one of the top GIS systems used by scientists. Natalie presented her salmon shark research at an ArcGIS convention. She was the youngest presenter there!

MATLAB stands for "matrix laboratory." It has many uses in technical computing for scientists and engineers. It integrates data and visuals, showing data in mathematical forms, developing algorithms, and creating models and graphics. Universities often use MATLAB in mathematics, engineering, and science programs.

Research topics can be expensive, so funding is necessary. Natalie applied for and received large grants from Stanford for two projects while working on her degrees.

Living Atlas

The ArcGIS community has developed a living atlas of the world. What is the difference between a living map and a regular map? Why are living maps useful? You can look at many maps at this website. Which maps are the most useful to you? Do any of the maps look more like art than data?

ArcGIS living map 🔍

One of these projects was "Dive Behavior Analysis of the Great White Shark in the Northeastern Pacific" in 2010. A year later, she received a grant for "Spatial and Temporal Analysis of Salmon Shark Migration in the California Current."

Because so many marine biology jobs are connected to universities, there is a strong emphasis on getting many papers published. Having your research work published in scientific journals is one of the things that many employers look for when hiring marine biologists.

TAGGING

For the type of research Natalie does, animals are often tagged. One of the best ways to get data and information is by tagging marine animals with electronic sensors. Once the creatures are tagged, satellites from space transmit data from those sensors for marine biologists to study and analyze.

Although there are different types of tags, they all provide information about where, when, and how marine life travels in the ocean.

Ask & Answer

Why is data so important in marine biology?

Satellites and Tagging

Satellites are being used more often in marine science. Data can be downloaded from the satellite. Learn more about how tagging works here.

Pop-up satellite tags 🔍

A pop-up satellite tag (PSAT)
photo credit: DesertStarSystem

Tagging has led to many discoveries. One discovery is that some species use specific "marine highways" when they migrate.

Some types of tags often either come loose from an animal or the animal must be recaptured so marine biologists can retrieve the data directly from the tags. Tags that detach from animals can often be returned to scientists for rewards.

Natalie prepares tags and equipment and also works on photographic documentations. She has been involved in tagging bluefin tuna and great white sharks. Her research group's great white shark research, "Eating or meeting? Cluster analysis reveals intricacies of white shark migration and offshore behavior," has also been published in an academic journal, *PLOS One*.

The research team used pop-up archival transmitting (PAT) tags to analyze migration patterns and to look at different diving behaviors of great white sharks. The illustration below, published in their article, shows different diving behaviors based on location. Each color represents one of five different clusters of sharks tagged for the study.

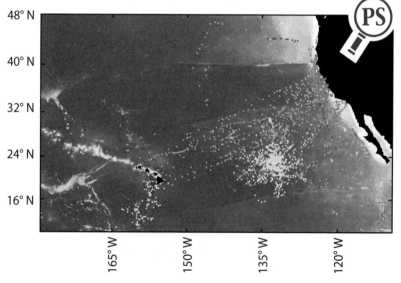

Diagram from Natalie's published research, revealing different diving behaviors of great white sharks off the coast of California.

photo credit: ©2012 Jorgensen et al.

ART AND SCIENCE

Along the way to her marine biology degrees, Natalie's artistic side was awakened. It's not too surprising when you realize that she often spent time in her father's art studio while growing up. Like her father, Natalie paints. She started painting in college by accident. She didn't mean to have a second career as an artist, but when she began oil painting, it just took off.

A New York curator noticed one of Natalie's paintings hanging in her dad's studio and wanted to put it in a show. She has been exhibiting her art ever since in galleries and art shows. Although she has had some success as a professional artist, she insists that she would paint regardless because it's such a source of joy.

Large-scale paintings put Natalie on a ladder as she fills the canvas with hazy, often monochromatic images that seem like something you would see in a dream. Although the ocean inspires her, it isn't always her subject. Instead, her subjects range from lightning to gas stations.

Malibu Magazine says that she brings a "scientist's eye to American painting." Always, her art represents the environment as she sees it. So far, humans haven't appeared on her canvases.

Art in the Ocean

Art of the ocean is nothing new, but how about art IN the ocean? Not only is it possible, but it serves a useful purpose in ecosystems. See how these underwater sculptures are enjoyed by humans and marine life.

Jason deCaires Taylor TED talk 🔍

More often, her paintings address climate change. Natalie firmly believes that you can't study marine biology without studying climate change.

Both science and art allow Natalie to creatively express herself, but they also help her understand and find the truth. Science and art are alike in many ways. You start with an idea, question, or problem. You find an answer through creative problem solving or the scientific process.

Ask & Answer

Natalie feels there is a synergy, or connection, between art and science. On the surface, they appear very different. Have you ever had two interests that seem very different, but have a similar kind of affect on you?

> 66 Both processes, science and art, are a form of exploration, at once both highly emotional and analytical, but always inquisitive. The methods might be different, but the goal is the same—seeking truth in the most authentic way I know how. 99
>
> **—Natalie Arnoldi**

Kathryn Sullivan

NOAA is a federal government agency that studies, monitors, and manages policy about the atmosphere and oceans. Leading NOAA is Kathryn Sullivan (1951–), a member of NASA's first female astronaut class and the first American woman to walk in space. Before she walked in space, this deep-sea geologist explored the ocean depths. After retiring from NASA, Kathy returned to her love of oceanography as a scientist for NOAA, before being appointed NOAA administrator and under secretary of commerce for oceans and atmosphere. You can hear her talk about living on a planet of oceans here. She says, "No matter what you see out your living room window or off of your back porch, you are first and foremost a citizen of the planet—and a citizen of an ocean planet."

Kathryn Sullivan
Earth Is Blue 🔎

THE FUTURE OF MARINE BIOLOGY

In late 2015, Natalie spent a few months at Hopkins Marine Station working as a research team coordinator for the filming of great white sharks of the California Current for the Discovery Channel television show, *Shark Week*. Natalie's job was to make certain they accurately represented the shark research on the Northeast Pacific great white shark population.

In her study of marine predators, such as sharks, Natalie has learned that their presence says a lot about the ecological health of the waters. Sharks are known as apex predators. Other apex predators in the ocean are marlins and tuna.

This means that they are at the top of the food chain and eat only meat. Sharks consume other creatures, including smaller fish and marine mammals. Sharks have no ocean predators that dine upon them.

66 It is important that we, as scientists, study all aspects of marine biology so we can predict what might happen and perhaps try to reverse or at least decrease impacts we have made on our world. 99

—Stasia Ferbey,
biologist and "clam expert"
at Biologica Environmental Services Ltd.

Cool Careers:
Marine Conservationists and Marine Ecologists

Marine conservationists work on the protection and preservation of marine ecosystems, while balancing the needs of people and nature.

Marine ecologists study how marine animals interact with their environments. Like marine conservationists, marine ecologists may work on solving problems or repairing damage.

In 2010, the worst oil spill in U.S. history occurred 42 miles off the coast of Louisiana. More than 130 million gallons of oil leaked into the ocean. Marine ecologists were some of the many people who arrived to do what they could to save marine life and coastal ecosystems.

The 2010 Deepwater Horizon oil spill, as seen from space

photo credit: NASA

Weather barometers measure atmospheric pressure and help predict the weather. Natalie believes sharks and other marine predators are barometers of the ocean. When there is a healthy population of predators, then the system is doing well. If there are too many or too few, then there are or will be problems in the system.

Humans tend to be the top predator of the ocean food chain, eating its top predators, such as tuna, halibut, and swordfish. With the human population climbing to 8 billion people in the near future, the ocean will be increasingly important as a source of food and other resources.

Natalie's future in marine biology will most likely include pursuing a PhD, which she hopes to start in the fall of 2017. To be successful, Natalie believes you must be passionately interested in what you study. While her interest in the ocean was sparked by living close to it, the more Natalie learns, the more she wants to know about the ocean.

66 Studying marine science, particularly at the college level, is not easy. Having a deep love for the subject is what makes the challenges so rewarding. 99

—Natalie Arnoldi

Timeline

1769
- The last Steller's sea cow, a marine mammal in the North Pacific Ocean, is killed by European fur traders.

1807
- President Thomas Jefferson authorizes a survey of the coastline.

1843
- Edward Forbes (1815–1854), believed to be the first modern-day marine biologist, theorizes that different ocean animals lived at different depths. This proves to be true. He also states that nothing lives below 1,800 feet, which is later proven false.

1872–1876
- The *Challenger* expedition circumnavigates the globe in the first oceanographic research expedition. Hundreds of new species and underwater mountains are discovered.

1882
- The *Albatross*, the first oceanographic research vessel built by a government, begins operations.

1914
- Acoustic exploration of the oceans begins.

1917–1919
- Oceanic acoustic research is developed by the U.S. Navy and Army Coast Artillery to detect enemy submarines during World War I.

1923–1928
- All coast survey ships are equipped with deep-water acoustic sounding instruments.

1934
- William Beebe (1877–1962) is lowered in a tethered bathysphere to a depth of 3,028 feet in the first manned underwater exploration.

1943
- Jacques Cousteau (1910–1997) develops modern-day scuba equipment that uses breathing regulators.

1954
- The first untethered research submersible is operated by French researchers.

1957
- Marie Tharp (1920–2006) creates the first scientific map of the ocean floor.

1961

- Scripps Institution of Oceanography develops a deep tow system, which is the forerunner of all remotely operated and unmanned oceanographic systems.

1962

- Rachel Carson's (1907–1964) book, *Silent Spring*, is published.

1964

- *Alvin*, created by Woods Hole Oceanographic Institution, is the first U.S.-based deep-diving submersible.

1965

- *Sealab II*, an underwater habitat, is lowered off the coast of California.

1970

- Sylvia Earle (1935–) leads the first team of female aquanauts to live and work in an underwater habitat, for the Tektite Project. She also sets a record for solo diving to a depth of 1,000 meters.

- National Oceanic & Atmospheric Administration (NOAA) is formed.

1971

- Ruth Turner (1914–2000) is the first woman to participate in a research voyage in *Alvin*.

1977

- Hydrothermal vents and an ecosystem that survives without the energy of the sun are discovered.

1982

- NOAA's Pacific Marine Environmental Laboratory installs an oceanographic buoy array to aid in predictions of El Niño events.

1990

- Marine biologist Cindy Van Dover (1954–) becomes the first female pilot of *Alvin*.

1995

- Declassification of GEOSAT satellite radar leads to the first worldwide mapping of the seafloor.

2010

- The first-ever Census of Marine Life catalogs the diversity, abundance, and distribution of marine species collected in an online database.

Ask & Answer

Introduction

- Why is marine biology an important career for women and men? What would science be like if only one gender worked at it?

Chapter 1

- If you lived hundreds of years ago and saw a creature with 10 arms and giant eyeballs, what would you have thought?

- In the early days of marine biology, many animals were removed from their habitats and ecosystems and destroyed, so people could learn about new species. Do you think the results justify the methods? What would you have done?

- How do scientists decide when a deep-sea expedition is worth the risk? What do they do to make it as safe as possible?

- Many marine animals are on the endangered list, and some, such as Steller's sea cow, are now extinct. What do you think the role of marine biologists should be in conservation?

Chapter 2

- What conditions do you think need to happen for larvae to successfully develop into adult marine life?

- Have you ever seen an intertidal tide pool? What do you think happens to the animals in it when the tide comes in and then goes out?

- What do you think is meant by the earth being the field site for marine scientists? Can other scientists say the same thing? What other sciences have the earth as its field site?

- Women who are pioneers in their fields often state they feel a responsibility to the women who come after them. Why do you think this happens?

- Sometimes, scientists have to quickly change their plans to make the most of unexpected opportunities. What are other times that this is an important skill? Do you ever do this in your life?

Ask & Answer

Chapter 3

- Is it helpful to meet someone when you're young who is interested in things you might be interested in? Why or why not?

- Marine biology wasn't what Ashanti expected, but she found a way to pursue her dream through marine chemistry. Have you ever been disappointed about something you were looking forward to? What did you do?

- Have you heard of situations where contaminants in water made people or animals sick? What do you think should be done when this happens?

- It was almost the beginning of the twenty-first century when Ashanti graduated from Texas A&M. Why do you think there hadn't been an African American oceanography graduate before her?

- Can you think of some examples of institutional racism? What are some ways to stop or reduce it?

Chapter 4

- A mentor is a knowledgeable person who advises someone, just as Barbara advised Natalie. Have you ever had a mentor? If so, how did your mentor help you?

- Why is data so important in marine biology?

- Natalie feels there is a synergy, or connection, between art and science. On the surface, they appear very different. Have you ever had two interests that seem very different, but have a similar kind of effect on you?

97

Glossary

abundant: a large amount.

acidification: in the ocean, the condition of increased carbon dioxide and lowered pH and oxygen.

adapt: to make changes to cope with your environment.

anthropology: the study of human culture and human development.

apex predator: a predator at the top of a food chain that has no creatures preying on it.

aquatic: living or growing in water.

atmosphere: the mixture of gases surrounding the earth.

bacteria: one-celled organisms.

barometer: an instrument that measures atmospheric pressure.

bathysphere: a manned chamber for deep-sea observation, which is lowered by a cable from a ship.

benthic: organisms that live on the seafloor.

biodiversity: the condition in nature in which a wide variety of species live in a single area.

biogeochemical: when chemical elements are transferred between living systems and the environment.

biological oceanography: the study of life and processes in the oceans.

biologist: a scientist who studies life.

biology: a branch of science that studies living things.

biotechnology: the use of organisms to make useful products.

cannery: a factory where food is canned.

census: an official count or survey of a population.

chemical oceanography: the study of ocean chemistry and the behavior of chemical elements in water.

chemistry: the science of the properties of substances and how substances react with one another.

chemosynthesis: the process of bacteria using energy from chemicals to combine water and carbon dioxide to produce carbohydrates.

circumnavigate: to sail around or fly around, usually the earth.

classify: to put things in groups based on what they have in common.

climate change: the long-term change in earth due to increased atmospheric temperature.

colony: a population of plants or animals of one species that lives in a particular place.

conservation: managing and protecting natural resources.

contaminant: any physical, chemical, biological, or radiological substance or matter in water.

coral: an animal with a hard outer calcium carbonate skeleton.

coral reef: a formation of coral in which parts have solidified.

crustacean: a group of marine animals that includes crabs, lobsters, shrimps, and barnacles.

data: information from tests or experiments.

diversity: a range of different things.

ecology: the study of the relationship between organisms and their environment.

economics: the material welfare of humankind.

Glossary

ecosystem: a community of living and nonliving things and their environment. Living things are plants, animals, and insects. Nonliving things are soil, rocks, and water.

El Niño: the flow of unusually warm water along the western coast of South America that causes changes in weather in other places.

endangered: when a species is in danger of becoming extinct.

engineer: someone who uses science, math, and creativity to design and build things.

environment: a natural area with animals, plants, rocks, soil, and water.

estuary: a partly enclosed coastal body of water connected to the ocean, which has rivers and streams flowing into it, where saltwater and freshwater mix together.

evolution: changing or developing slowly over time. Evolution is the theory of how species develop from earlier forms of life and the belief that humans evolved from lower orders of animals.

extinct: when a group of plants or animals dies out and there are no more left in the world.

fieldwork: work done by personal observation.

fishery: a place where fish are raised or grown for commercial purposes.

food chain: a community of animals and plants where each is eaten by another higher up in the chain.

fossil fuels: coal, oil, natural gas—fuel made from the fossils of plants and animals that lived millions of years ago.

fluid dynamics: the science of fluids in motion.

forensic: determining or examining the cause of death or injury.

gender: male or female.

genetics: the study of genes and heredity. Genes are basic units in our cells that carry characteristics from one generation to the next.

geology: the study of the history and physical nature of the earth.

GIS: Geographic Information System. A system that can be used for mapping.

global warming: an increase in the average temperature of the earth's atmosphere, enough to cause climate change.

gravity: a force that pulls all objects toward the earth.

greenhouse gas: a gas in the atmosphere that traps heat.

habitat: the natural area where a plant or an animal lives.

half-life: time for a specific property to decrease in half; in science, refers to radioactivity.

horizontal: parallel or being on the same level as the ground or horizon.

hydrophone: a microphone that detects sound waves in the ocean.

hydrothermal: heated underground water.

ichthyologist: a scientist who studies fish.

inquisitive: intellectual curiosity or asking questions.

institutional racism: a pattern of social institutions such as government or schools giving negative treatment to a group of people based on race.

Glossary

larva: an organism at the beginning stage of development. Plural is larvae.

life cycle: the growth and changes a living thing goes through, from birth to death.

mammals: a class of animals that includes humans. These animals have backbones, nourish their young with milk, and are mostly covered with hair. Humans, dogs, horses, whales, and mice are mammals.

mammalogist: a scientist who studies mammals.

marine: found in the ocean or having to do with the ocean.

marine biological station: a field station or laboratory where marine scientists conduct research and experiments.

marine biology: the study of life in the water.

marsh: a wet, lowland area.

mentor: an experienced and trusted advisor.

meteorology: the study of weather and climate.

microbes: a huge variety of living creatures that are so small they can be seen only with a microscope.

microorganism: a single-cell organism that can be seen only with a microscope.

microscopic: something so small that it can be seen only with a microscope.

migration: the seasonal movement of animals.

minerals: naturally occurring solids found in rocks and in the ground. Rocks are made of minerals.

modification: a change.

mollusk: an animal with a soft body protected by a shell, such as a clam or snail.

monochromatic: containing only one color.

naturalist: someone who studies plants and animals in nature.

nautical: pertaining to the ocean, navigation, or ships.

Northern Hemisphere: the half of the earth north of the equator.

nuclear fission: a reaction in which the nucleus of an atom splits, resulting in the release of energy.

oceanographer: a scientist who studies the ocean.

oceanography: a branch of science that studies the ocean.

organism: any living thing, such as a plant or animal.

pesticide: a substance used to destroy pests harmful to people, animals, or plants.

photosynthesis: the process a plant goes through to make its own food. The plant uses water and carbon dioxide in the presence of sunlight to make oxygen and sugar.

physical oceanography: the study of the physical processes and properties of the ocean.

physics: the science of how matter and energy work together. Matter is what an object is made of. Energy is the ability to perform work.

picoplankton: organisms a fraction of the size of plankton, typically 0.2 to 2 micrometers.

plankton: organisms living in the water column.

predator: an animal that eats other animals.

Glossary

pressure: the force that pushes on any object.

radioactive: having or producing a powerful form of energy known as radioactivity.

radiogeochemistry: the study of radioactive elements in the environment.

radionuclide: an unstable chemical element that releases radiation.

regulator: in marine science, a device that controls the rate of oxygen for breathing.

Renaissance: a cultural rebirth focused on the arts, music, and literature occurring in Europe.

resource: something that people can use, such as water, food, and building materials.

respiration: a process in living organisms involving the production of energy, typically the intake of oxygen and the release of carbon dioxide.

rift zone: an area where tectonic plates are moving apart.

ROV: a remotely operated vehicle.

satellite: a device that orbits the earth to relay communication signals or transmit information.

scuba: stands for self-contained underwater breathing apparatus.

sediment: dirt, fertilizer, rocks, and other tiny bits of matter deposited in rivers and oceans.

shaman: a wise leader, who Native people believe has special powers and can connect with the spiritual world.

sensor: a device that measures and records physical properties.

spawn: to produce eggs or young.

species: a group of plants or animals that are closely related and produce offspring.

specimen: a sample of something.

submersible vessel: a boat that can go below the surface of the water.

sulfide: a substance that includes sulfur.

symbiotic: the relationship between two different kinds of living things that depend on each other.

tagging: attaching a sensor for the purpose of data collection.

technology: tools, methods, and systems used to solve a problem or do work.

theory: an unproven idea used to explain something.

thesis: a long piece of writing on a particular subject that is done to earn a degree at a university.

tectonic plates: large sections of the earth's crust that move on top of the hot, melted layer below.

tidal pool: a rocky pool on the seashore filled with saltwater at low tide.

tidal wetland: a wetland where seawater and freshwater mixes along coasts.

tide: the daily rising and falling of ocean water along the coast.

trawling: dragging and sifting with a net.

water column: the idea of the layers of the ocean with different features at different depths.

vent: an opening in the earth's crust.

vertical: up and down.

wetland: an area where the land is soaked with water, such as a marsh or swamp. Wetlands are often important habitats for fish, plants, and wildlife.

zoology: the study of animals.

Resources

Books

- *Sylvia Earle: Ocean Explorer (Women in Conservation).* Fertig, Dennis. Heinemann, 2014.
- *Marine Biology: An Introduction to Ocean Ecosystems.* Hill, Amy. J Weston Walch, 2002.
- *Citizens of the Sea: Wondrous Creatures from the Census of Marine Life.* Knowlton, Nancy. National Geographic, 2010.
- *You Can Be a Woman Marine Biologist.* McAlary, Florence and Cohen, Judith Love. Cascade Press, 2001.
- *Marine Biologists (Out of the Lab: Extreme Jobs in Science).* Owen, Ruth. Power Kids Press, 2013.
- *Fish Watching with Eugenie Clark.* Ross, Michael Elsohn. Carolrhoda Books, 2000.

Websites and Museums

- MarineBio: *marinebio.org*
- Marine Mammal Center: *marinemammalcenter.org/education/marine-mammal-information*
- Monterey Bay Aquarium: *montereybayaquarium.org*
- NASA, Climate Kids: *climatekids.nasa.gov/menu/ocean*
- National Aquarium: *aqua.org*
- National Geographic, The Ocean: *ocean.nationalgeographic.com/ocean*
- NOAA Kids Page: *oceanservice.noaa.gov/kids*
- NOAA Ocean Explorer: *oceanexplorer.noaa.gov*
- Oceanus Magazine: *whoi.edu/oceanus*
- Scripps Whale Acoustic Lab: *cetus.ucsd.edu*
- Women Oceanographers: *womenoceanographers.org*
- Woods Hole Oceanic Institution, Dive and Discover: *divediscover.whoi.edu*
- Smithsonian Museum of Natural History, Ocean Portal: *ocean.si.edu*

Resources

QR Code Glossary

- Page 2: yourshot.nationalgeographic.com/photos/2520250/?source=gallery
- Page 7: ted.com/talks/sylvia_earle_s_ted_prize_wish_to_protect_our_oceans
- Page 11: bradshawfoundation.com/bradshaws/kimberley3.php
- Page 13: ocean.si.edu/corals-and-coral-reefs
- Page 17: youtube.com/watch?v=JHOb_iqepuk
- Page 19: youtube.com/watch?v=N2qmf24O0yo
- Page 21: video.nationalgeographic.com/video/news/wild-chronicles/marine-census-wcvin?source=searchvideo
- Page 22: coml.org
- Page 26: climate.gov/teaching/resources/global-science-investigator
- Page 37: whoi.edu/about
- Page 46: climatekids.nasa.gov/ocean
- Page 48: worldoceansday.org
- Page 55: cbsnews.com/videos/the-price-of-progress
- Page 58: eyeofthewhaleresearch.org/gallery.html
- Page 66: youtube.com/watch?v=anrGN4MwD9Y
- Page 77: youtube.com/watch?v=1s6zy8SB3Is
- Page 82: ted.com/talks/barbara_block_tagging_tuna_in_the_deep_ocean
- Page 84: doc.arcgis.com/en/living-atlas/about
- Page 86: nmfs.noaa.gov/stories/2014/09/how_animals_see_the_ocean.html
- Page 89: ted.com/talks/jason_decaires_taylor_an_underwater_art_museum_teeming_with_life
- Page 90: sanctuaries.noaa.gov/earthisblue/wk52-dr-sullivan-earth-is-blue.html

Index

Index

Index